The Backward Christmas Pageant

Dennis Hartin

Abingdon Press

Nashville

THE BACKWARD CHRISTMAS PAGEANT

Copyright © 2003 by Abingdon Press

This book is printed on recycled, acid-free paper.

Scripture quotations in this publication are from the New Revised Standard Version of the Bible, copyright © 1989 by the Division of Christian Education of the National Council of the Churches of Christ in the USA.

ISBN 0-687-06476-7

04 05 06 07 08 09 10 11 12 — 10 9 8 7 6 5 4 3 2

MANUFACTURED IN THE UNITED STATES OF AMERICA

Contents

Introduction and Production Notes 4

Cast List 10

Prop and Costume List (Optional) 11

Prologue 13

Act 3 15

Act 2 19

Act 1, Scene 1 22

Act 1, Scene 2 25

Epilogue 27

Song Texts 29

Script Notes 33

Music

1. We Three Kings 37

2. Good Christian Friends, Rejoice 40

3. Sing We Now of Christmas 42

4. Rise Up, Shepherd, and Follow 44

5. O Come, All Ye Faithful 46

6. O Little Town of Bethlehem 48

7. Away in a Manger 50

8. Medley: On This Day / Joy to the World 52

CD Track List 56

Introduction and Production Notes

This pageant is designed for a production with no set, no budget, and no live musical accompaniment. If you have a set, budget, and/or live musical accompaniment, you can perform this pageant, too, but you'll have to be really careful, as we'll explain later. Cast members (and production staff) should be dressed to approximate shepherds, wise people, angels, and Bethlehem folk, scrounging up costumes and props. This script comes from the perspective that any attempt by poor, ornery people (like you and like me) to tell the story of God's grace can be only a poor shadow of the glory and mystery of God, no matter what kind of budget or special effects can be employed. With that in mind, approach the task as simply as possible, asking for God's grace, and expecting to be surprised.

Why We Go for Laughs

Voltaire said, "God is a comedian playing to an audience too afraid to laugh." Garrison Keillor said, "God writes comedy, it's just that he's stuck with actors who don't know how to play for laughs."

In the classic sense, the Christmas story is a comedy, or more accurately, the final act of a comedy. By comedy, I mean a story in which a relationship is established, then, through a series of misadventures, the relationship is endangered but is ultimately restored. Every romantic comedy has this structure, as do Shakespeare's comedies. In the Christmas story, all the confusion and all the tears culminate in God's grace among us.

And still, we're confused. We're expecting a king riding a chariot, with all the forces of heaven behind. We're getting a baby? OK, then it's a baby born in splendor. A baby born to an unwed mother? Oops. A baby born in a manger? OK, then, let's have the nation rejoice. Sorry, all you get are shepherds and some Magi from out of town.

Throughout the story, our expectations are dashed—but those are just *our* expectations. Throughout his narrative, Matthew cites Scripture to show that this topsy-turvy arrangement is what God had in mind all along. You say you don't have those expectations? You say you thought it would be the manger scene all along? I have two responses to that: (1) I don't believe you. We all expect God to go for the spectacle, because we think God has to impress us to make points. It could be that we think we have to impress God to make points, and we expect God to be like us. (2) You only have those expectations because you've heard the story a thousand times. As a result, you have stopped listening to the story. The absurdity of God's grace should jangle against the ear, which makes it more of a miracle. I am fortunate to have Jewish friends with whom I can talk about my faith, and they never fail to be confounded by the obvious incongruity of the Incarnation. Christians should be confounded by it too.

This pageant looks at the Christmas story from the point of view of the recipients of God's grace as they react with varying degrees of fear, awe, misunderstanding, and hostility.

Production Suggestions

Avoid auditions. A Christmas pageant is not a talent show. The last thing you want is competition. Cast performers with the advice of your assistant directors, or talk to Sunday school teachers before the first rehearsals about who might want to be in the pageant. If there are people you really want in the pageant, ask them. Ask everybody, in fact, and ask them in person.

Hold your scripts. During the pageant, the performers should hold their scripts and speak into microphones on stands. The reproducible script pages are designed to make this easy to accomplish. If you're one of the minority of directors with a pool of performers who memorize well and speak audibly in a large room, or a budget big enough for wireless mikes, ignore the previous sentence. For the rest of us, being onstage produces enough anxiety that holding a script in front of us allows us to relax and enjoy the production. If the idea of seeing all those scripts during the pageant drives you nuts, hide them in handheld props, such as scrolls or baskets. Remind the cast that the script they are holding is the net, not the trapeze. They must look up when they are speaking. It is very important

that the performers speak into the microphones so that the audience can hear the lines.

Look like a pageant. All adults, including ushers, have to dress for the event as shepherds, angels, or wise people. It will make it less obvious when an assistant director has to sneak onstage to give a cue or pick something up. At least as important, dressing the adults give the cast the sense that everyone is in this together.

How to Run a Survivable Rehearsal

This pageant is written in three acts, with a prologue and an epilogue. With the exception of the Rookie Shepherd and the possible exception of the Sheep (see Script Notes), no cast member appears in more than one act. Everyone is in the prologue and the epilogue. **This makes it possible to rehearse all three acts simultaneously.** The reason for this becomes clear when you recall the typical Christmas pageant rehearsal.

Imagine a traditional, three-section, forty-five-minute (including music) pageant script, with Joseph and Mary featured up to the arrival at the inn, then the scene with the shepherds, then the wise people. There may be dialogue between a shepherd and Mary, or the wise people may have a scene with Joseph. Every so often, the group breaks into song. This scenario requires every performer to be available for every part of the rehearsal, with a lot of downtime during rehearsal. Downtime often means kids disrupting the rehearsal or wandering around the church building.

I solved this problem by writing the pageant so that all three acts could be rehearsed simultaneously. (In this pageant, only one cast member appears in more that one act.) With the three acts rehearsed in this way, it is best to have separate narrators for each act, in addition to Narrator 1 and Narrator 2. If a production is shorthanded, Narrator 1 and Narrator 2 could each double "Act One Narrator," "Act Two Narrator," and "Act Three Narrator." That is, Narrator 1 could narrate Act One, Narrator 2 could narrate Act Two, and someone else could narrate Act Three. These suggestions can be adapted as needed based on your unique situation.

An Example of How It Works

First, the director should plan all the blocking for the characters. Using a simple system of X's and O's for each of the characters, draw a blocking chart for each act of the pageant. Keep the blocking simple, focusing especially on getting people on and off the stage without traffic jams. Make copies for assistant directors.

Second, hold a meeting with at least three assistant directors a few days before the first rehearsal. If there are more than three people who want to help, put someone in charge of finding props and setting them up where they are needed, and put another helper in charge of finding and/or approving costumes. Each assistant director is responsible for rehearsing one act of the pageant. Read through the script and give each director the blocking for the act he or she will direct. Discuss technical issues, such as where microphones will be placed, where the cast will rehearse, who will handle light-

ing and sound, and so on.

1. At the first rehearsal, everyone assembles in the sanctuary, and the director and assistants gather names. The music director spends ten minutes or so teaching the cast any song the entire cast needs to know, such as the closing number.

2. At the same time, the director meets in the back of the sanctuary to make casting decisions with the assistant directors, based on who is present. When the music director is finished, the names of the cast are read, along with the name of the assistant director who will rehearse each group.

3. The assistant directors for Act Two and Act Three find separate locations in the church building to hand out scripts and to rehearse blocking and lines. The director begins the rehearsal with the Act One cast, going through blocking and lines.

4. After twenty-five minutes, the assistant director for Act Two brings his or her group back to the sanctuary. The Act One cast leaves with their assistant director and reviews their blocking and lines in another part of the church.

5. Twenty-five minutes later, the assistant director for Act Three brings his or her group to the sanctuary. The Act Two group leaves the sanctuary to review what they have done.

Instead of rehearsing a forty-five-minute pageant in which each cast member spends most of the time waiting to rehearse, have three rehearsals of three short scenes, in which each cast member has work to do nearly all the time. Cast members have less time to get bored and into mischief and they are more comfortable during the performance, since they have spent more time actually rehearsing.

The music director assigns and rehearses the music separately from the rest of the production weeks before the two rehearsals described here. The people performing the music should not also be part of the dramatic cast in the three acts, to ensure that each part of the pageant can be rehearsed separately. If the rotating sessions in the sanctuary go well, add a quick run-through at the end of the first two-hour rehearsal. Alternately, the director can go from room to room as the three acts rehearse.

The timeline shows a possible two-hour rehearsal, including where each group meets and the duration of each rehearsal. If your cast will be memorizing the script, use the same model and add more rehearsals, as needed. If you need more time for one act, appropriate five minutes from the act rehearsing in the sanctuary and five minutes from the run-through time to focus attention on the act that needs more work.

The second rehearsal is a straight run-through with music. Remember to watch the clock, and to skip over parts that are already well rehearsed. Make sure that all cast members know when they have an entrance. Since the cast will be holding scripts, the director's main job is traffic control. As much as is possible, place an assistant wherever a character will make an entrance. An assistant can sit with the wise people, rookie shepherd, angel, and the sheep to cue them when to speak or when to enter.

Musical Notes

- **Don't have the congregation sing.** This allows you to keep the lights over the congregation low, and gives them the sense that they are at an "event," rather than a service of worship.

- **Don't do the old standbys, unless you can find new ways to present them.** The music suggestions and the enclosed CD offer you a few new songs and a few familiar songs to sing in a new way. The one exception to this rule: The kids in second grade and younger always have an ensemble title and sing "Away in a Manger." There are two reasons for this: (1) Parents really like it. If they're put off by anything else in the pageant, we can get forgiveness by having the little ones sing; and (2) I like it!

	10 Minutes	25 Minutes	25 Minutes	25 Minutes	35 Minutes
Sanctuary	ALL	Act One	Act Two	Act Three	ALL (Run-through)
Room A		Act Two	Act One	Act One	
Room B		Act Three	Act Three	Act Two	

About This Edition

The package you hold in your hands is designed so that any church can produce a pageant. If you don't have a live accompanist, you can play the enclosed CD accompaniment for the songs. If you do have an accompanist, use the CD for the sound effects. You can also use music that is not included here if you prefer.

This pageant is not about you. Or your church. Or even the kids in your church. It is about God's grace among us and our reaction to that grace. One way we confound God's grace is by taking ourselves too seriously—that was certainly Herod's problem. Resist the temptation to do something *with* or *to* the script just to show how clever or talented you (or the performers) are. Resist the urge to punch up the script to get bigger laughs. In comedy, as in life, bigger is not always better. Resist the urge to add production values simply for the sake of looking more dramatic or professional. There is nothing quite so lame as trying to recreate the grandeur of God through our little human efforts, no matter how big a budget you can muster. Ask yourself this question as often as you need to: "Are we doing this because we are trying to make God's grace more apparent to the audience, or are we just trying to show off how clever and talented we are?"

Whatever you do, you should do as well as you can, secure in God's grace. Speaking of grace, I should include a word about "flubs." Nearly every "cute" pageant story is about some kid muffing a line or missing an entrance. Allow your performers the chance for memorable moments of excellence, rather than having their miscues tell the story. Show them that you respect them, as well as the story being told.

The Nativity is a story of people who don't know how to act in the light of God's grace. We are these people. This is a children's story, not just because we associate Christmas with children, but because they are a perfect vehicle for material showing equal parts trepidation and boldness in the face of circumstances both comforting and challenging. That is the nature of theater and the nature of the gospel. This pageant is intended as a re-creation, not just a retelling, of the Nativity story. It is the task of the directors, actors, musicians, and all to proclaim God's grace and expect a response. The response, of course, comes from the audience. It is a simple story. Stay out of its way.

Author's Note: Of Time and the Baby

In the summer of 2001, I was struggling to come up with a way to present the Christmas story that would make people feel they were hearing it for the first time. I ruminated over the idea of telling the story backward—starting with the wise people's encounter with Herod, then to the announcement by the angel to the shepherds, and then to the story of Mary and Joseph. The notion came from a musical I had seen years before, *Merrily We Roll Along,* in which the life of the protagonist is traced beginning in 1980 and ending in 1955. Giving that treatment to the Nativity would have the effect of beginning with the political ramifications of Jesus' birth in the Herod scene, and ending with the personal stories of Mary and Joseph. It looked to me like a movie with a wide establishing shot of a crowd at the beginning, then the camera slowly zooming into the faces of just a couple in the crowd. An interesting idea, I thought, but does it tell the story?

By the fall of 2001, I was struggling to come up with a way to present the Christmas story in a way that would make people want to hear it in a time that had gone crazy. Our church is in a community in the suburbs of New York City; there would be people in the congregation who had escaped the World Trade Center, and people who knew others who did not.

"This will change everything," people were saying in those first days after the attack, and they were right. But I was telling a story about how the birth of Christ had changed things long ago, and how his birth continues to change things. How do I tell the story, I wondered, in a time that had gone crazy?

"Crazy time," I thought. And the idea of telling the story backward suddenly made sense. Part of the point would be that time doesn't matter in this story. The birth of a

baby two thousand years ago can be of more import than this year's tragedy. This is not to minimize death; it is to remember the timelessness of God's grace.

"This will change everything," is how I ended the pageant. The story of our redemption, begun in Christ's birth, is always before and ahead of current events.

A lot of people conspire to make this and other pageants I've worked on come to life. They are due credit for being good storytellers in their own right. Thank you, Melissa Barisch, Charlene Cosman, Anita D'Amico, Linda Dickman, Kim Gilbert, Nancy Hogan, Debbie Jenks, Tim Jenks, Roger Sherman, Pegge Strella, Joanne Taylor, Jerry Ulrich, and all the people I missed. Extra hugs to my wife, Peg Fox, who endures my creative temperament, and to our son, Sam Fox-Hartin, who is forever supplying me with gags. I hope one day to actually use one.

Grace and peace to you,

Dennis Hartin

The Backward Christmas Pageant was first performed December 16, 2001 at the First Presbyterian Church of Northport, New York.

Cast List

Prologue
Narrator 1
Narrator 2
Voice 1
Voice 2

Act Three
Sign Holder
Act Three Narrator
Sheep
Assistant
Wise Person 1
Wise Person 2
Wise Person 3
Wise Person 4
Prop Person (no lines)
Voice Offstage
Herod

Act Two
Sign Holder
Act Two Narrator
Sheep
Rookie Shepherd
Shepherd 1
Shepherd 2
Optional: Extra Shepherds (nonspeaking)
Angel
Angel Chorus

Act One
Sign Holder
Act One Narrator
Joseph
Mary
Angel
Rookie Shepherd

Epilogue
Narrator 1
Mary
Joseph
Narrator 2
Shepherd 1
Rookie Shepherd
Wise Person 1
Wise Person 4

(Notes: Voice 1 and Voice 2 can come from the back of the sanctuary, or from the back row of the cast. Any interested person, adult or child, can play these roles. The Sign Holder can be the same person for all three acts if needed. The Rookie Shepherd appears in two scenes. See Script Notes on page 33 for additional options on Sheep and Angel Chorus, Shepherds, and for casting the Wise People.)

Prop and Costume List

This is a list of props necessary to perform the script that follows. It is not an exhaustive list of everything you may want to use. For instance, you could give some of the shepherds crooks so that they look a little more like shepherds. Costumes are always a fun addition. Remember that the cast may be holding their scripts as they perform, so trying to juggle a script and extra props may be more than your cast will be able to do.

PROPS

ACT THREE
- Sign reading "ACT THREE"
- Telescope
- Three gift coverings (small towels or pieces of fabric)
- Gold (box wrapped in gold paper or spray painted gold with glued on beads, buttons, trim, and so on, if desired)
- Frankincense (small bottle filled with herbs)
- Soccer ball or other piece of sports equipment*
- Myrrh (small bottle filled with colored liquid)
- Large balls of lint (large cotton balls)*

---

*See Script Notes, page 33.

ACT TWO
- Sign reading "ACT TWO"
- Fake peanut butter sandwiches: You don't want to use real ones; they get unsanitary very quickly. Create fake sandwiches by using thick foam core or foam rubber sandwich-shaped rectangles that have been painted brown (or brown and purple) around the edges. (One for each shepherd.)
- Brown paper bags (whatever you have on hand to use as lunch bags)

ACT ONE
- Sign reading "ACT ONE"
- Two pieces of mail that can simulate letters*
- One green card*
- Brown paper lunch bag
- Fake peanut butter sandwich
- Optional: Large scraps of fabric for Rookie Shepherd's rag pile

COSTUMES

Simple, biblical costumes are appropriate for most of the cast. The basic costume is an oversized long-sleeved tunic that is usually worn with a fabric belt or cord. Head coverings can be made by folding a square of cloth diagonally with the fold across the forehead and a cord tied around the head to hold the head covering in place.

Sandals are worn by both men and women. Adapt the costume based on the character.

Narrators, Sign Holders, and Herod's Assistant wear simple, calf-length tunics in solid colors, and plain sandals on their feet. The Shepherds wear undyed, natural fabrics, such as muslin or linen. The Angel's tunic should be white and ankle-length. Mary's robe is traditionally in blue. Joseph wears a long tunic and a cloak in plain neutral-colored fabric. The Wise People would be dressed in finer fabrics in rich colors, such as purple, red, or royal blue, with elaborate head coverings and jewelry. Herod would wear a long robe with a cloak, a crown, large rings, and other elaborate jewelry. All other cast members can wear plain tunics or robes with simple fabric headcoverings and sandals. Sheep can wear oversized white T-shirts or sweatshirts and "Sheep Caps" (see sidebar).

SHEEP CAPS

Materials Needed
- ❏ White ball caps
- ❏ Black felt
- ❏ Jumbo cotton balls
- ❏ Hot glue gun
- ❏ Black ball caps (opt.)
- ❏ Black pom-poms (opt.)

- Cut eyes, nose, and ears out of black felt.
- Glue eyes and nose onto the brim of the hat.
- Lay the ears across the top of the hat. Glue the ends and flip the ears over so they curl over the top of the hat.
- Glue cotton balls onto the entire crown of the hat.
- For a black sheep, use black pom-poms on a black ball cap.

Prologue

1 ♫ **"BETHLEHEM JOURNEY"** (CD #1, INSTRUMENTAL PRELUDE)

2

3 *(All performers are in the chancel area except* **Wise People 1, 2, 3,** *and* **4, Herod, Rookie**

4 **Shepherd, Angel,** *and* **Sheep.** *The* **Angel Chorus** *and other musicians are sitting near the*

5 *front.* **Narrator 1** *steps downstage center.)*

6

7 **NARRATOR 1:** In the name of our Savior, Jesus Christ, and on behalf of [*insert*

8 *name of your church*], I welcome you to this year's Christmas pageant.

9   Let us pray: Our Lord and God, let us tell your story faithfully and hear it joy-

10   fully. In Jesus' name, Amen.

11   Ladies and Gentlemen, I think you're going to really enjoy the . . .

12 **NARRATOR 2:** *(Interrupting)* Excuse me, but . . .

13 **NARRATOR 1:** . . . pageant . . . *(Somewhat irritated.)* Is something *wrong?*

14 **NARRATOR 2:** There's a little problem.

15 **NARRATOR 1:** If it's a *little* problem, you can fix it.

16 **NARRATOR 2:** OK, maybe it's *not* so little.

17 **NARRATOR 1:** We're just about to start the pageant, and then we're all having

18   dinner. Is this something that can . . . ?

19 **NARRATOR 2:** *(Interrupting)* . . . wait? No. It's one of the wise people.

20 **NARRATOR 1:** What about one of the wise people?

21 **NARRATOR 2:** He has to leave early.

22 **NARRATOR 1:** Leave early? What for?

23 **NARRATOR 2:** He didn't say. I think it's a soccer game.

24 **NARRATOR 1:** He can't leave early. The wise people are in the third act.

25 **NARRATOR 2:** I know, but I think we can still do this.

26 **NARRATOR 1:** Really? How?

27 **NARRATOR 2:** We just do the pageant backward.

28 **NARRATOR 1:** Sounds good. *(Pause)* We just do the pageant—*backward?*

29 **NARRATOR 2:** It'll be easy. We'll do the third act first and the first act third.

30 **NARRATOR 1:** *(Slowly)* We do the . . .

31 **NARRATOR 2:** . . . third act first and the first act third. Get it?

32 **NARRATOR 1:** Got it.

33 **NARRATOR 2:** Good. OK, everybody! Everybody! Listen up! Herod, wise people!

34   You're on first!

35 **VOICE 1:** What's on second?

36 **NARRATOR 2:** Shepherds. Mary and Joseph are on third. Everyone got that?

37 **VOICE 2:** Who's on first?

38 **NARRATOR 2:** No, Herod's on first!

39 **NARRATOR 1:** Time to start!

40 **NARRATOR 2:** Of course! *(Very dramatically)* Friends, we present *The Backward*

41   *Christmas Pageant!*

42

43  **"WE THREE KINGS" (CD #2, MUSIC PAGE 37)**

     The Backward Christmas Pageant

Act Three

1  **OPTIONAL: "BETHLEHEM JOURNEY," SHORT VERSION (CD #3)**

2

3 (**Sign Holder** *holds up the "ACT THREE" card. Play optional music as the "ACT THREE"*

4 *card is displayed.* **Sheep** *move quietly into place in the aisles.* **Assistant** *moves into place*

5 *onstage.*)

6

7 **ACT THREE NARRATOR:** Now when Jesus was born in Bethlehem of Judea in the

8   days of Herod the king, behold, wise people from the East came to Jerusalem,

9   saying, "Where is he who is born king of the Jews? For we have seen his star in

10   the East, and have come to worship him." Herod summoned the wise men

11   secretly and ascertained from them what time the star appeared and he sent

12   them to Bethlehem saying, "Go and search diligently for the child, and when

13   you have found him bring me word, so that I too may come and worship him."

14

15 (**Sheep** *"baa" in aisle.*)

16

17 **OPTIONAL: SHEEP SOUND EFFECT (CD #4)**

18

19 (*Fade sheep sounds as* **Wise Person 1** *speaks the next line.*)

20

21 **WISE PERSON 1:** (*From the back of the sanctuary or the side of the chancel area*) Excuse

22   me, is this the palace of King Herod?

23 **ASSISTANT:** Yes, it is.

24 **WISE PERSON 2:** King Herod, the mighty?

25 **ASSISTANT:** Indeed.

26 **WISE PERSON 3:** King Herod, the powerful?

27 **ASSISTANT:** Certainly.

28 **WISE PERSON 4:** Then, what are all these sheep doing here?

29

30 (**Sheep** *withdraw.*)

31

32 **OPTIONAL: SHEEP SOUND EFFECT (CD #4)**

33   (*Bring up the sheep "baa" volume slightly and then fade away.*)

34

35 **ASSISTANT:** Haven't got a clue. They've been wandering the streets all morning. I
36   was twenty minutes late for work. Blasted herd of sheep!
37 **WISE PERSON 1:** What's that?
38 **ASSISTANT:** Herd of sheep.
39 **WISE PERSON 2:** Of course, we've heard of sheep.
40 **ASSISTANT:** No, a *herd* of sheep. That's what caused the traffic jam.
41 **WISE PERSON 3:** Properly speaking, it's a flock.
42 **ASSISTANT:** A what?
43 **WISE PERSON 3:** A flock. The correct term for a group of sheep is a *flock*.
44 **ASSISTANT:** Who is that back there?
45 **WISE PERSON 3:** It is I.
46 **ASSISTANT:** Oh, an English major.
47
48 (**Wise People** *move to the center of the chancel area.*)
49
50
51 **OPTIONAL: "BETHLEHEM JOURNEY," SHORT VERSION (CD #3)**
52
53 (*Fade music as* **Wise Person 3** *speaks the next line.*)
54
55 **WISE PERSON 3:** I am a Wise Person from the East. I and my fellow Wise People
56   have come here, following yonder star.
57
58 (**Wise Person 3** *points to the star.* **Wise Person 2** *looks through the telescope as* **Wise Person
59 1** *and* **Wise Person 4** *create exaggerated postures of looking toward the star.*)
60 **ASSISTANT:** You know, we've been wondering what that was. Think it's got anything
61   to do with the sheep?
62 **WISE PERSON 2:** I don't believe so. (*Claps hands.* **Gift Bearers** *come forward with gifts,*
63   *hands them to* **Wise Persons 1, 2,** *and* **4.**) We have taken it as a sign that a king
64   has been born, and we have come to offer worship and give gifts.
65 **ASSISTANT:** Such as?
66 **WISE PERSON 1:** (*Revealing gift*) Gold!
67 **WISE PERSON 2:** (*Revealing gift*) Frankincense!
68 **WISE PERSON 4:** (*Revealing soccer ball*) Myrrh! *Oops!*
69
70 (**Prop Person** *comes out with a bottle filled with colored liquid, takes the soccer ball, and gives*
71 **Wise Person 4** *the bottle.*)
72
73 **WISE PERSON 4:** Thanks.

 The Backward Christmas Pageant

74 **VOICE OFFSTAGE:** The king approaches!

75

76 (**Herod** *enters through the center aisle, picking very large balls of lint off his clothing and*

77 *hair.*)

78

79 ♪ "KING HEROD'S ENTRANCE" (CD #5, INSTRUMENTAL)

80

81 *(Fade music as* **Herod** *nears the chancel.)*

82

83 **ASSISTANT:** Mighty king, what happened?

84 **HEROD:** Let's just say you pick up a lot of lint when you're in a traffic jam with

85   sheep. Who are *they? (Motions to the* **Wise People.***)*

86 **ASSISTANT:** Wise people from the East, your Highness. They seek a newborn king.

87 **HEROD:** This is news to me. Where did you hear about a newborn king?

88 **WISE PERSON 3:** Yonder star. (**Wise Person 3** *points to the star.* **Wise Person 2** *looks*

89   *through telescope as* **Wise Person 1** *and* **Wise Person 4** *create exaggerated postures of*

90   *looking toward the star.)* We take it as a sign.

91 **HEROD:** Oh, is that what it is? I thought it had something to do with the sheep.

92 **WISE PEOPLE** and **ASSISTANT:** *(Together)* We don't think so.

93 **HEROD:** I guess not. Look, will you fellows excuse us for a minute? I need to consult

94   with my staff on, uh, alternate side of the street shepherding. Just make your-

95   selves at home. While you're waiting, someone will perform a song appropri-

96   ate to the season.

97

98 (**Herod** *and* **Assistant** *move to the rear of the stage with their backs to the audience. They*

99 *mime talking together.)*

100

101

102 ♪ "GOOD CHRISTIAN FRIENDS, REJOICE" (CD #6, MUSIC PAGE 40)

103

104 *(As the music concludes,* **Herod** *and* **Assistant** *move to the front of the stage.)*

105

106 **HEROD:** Hope you enjoyed that.

107 **WISE PERSON 1:** Very much.

108 **HEROD:** We know you want to get on your way, so use the showers, pick up whatever

109   you want from the cafeteria, and go on your way to find that newborn king.

110   *BUT . . .* on your way home, I *insist* you stop here for the night, and when you

111   do, be sure to tell me where this king is, so I can eliminate him.

112

Act Three   **17**

113 (**Assistant** *stamps foot loudly.*)

114

115 **HEROD:** I mean, *worship* him. Did I say *eliminate?* I meant *worship!* Really!

116 **WISE PERSON 1:** Sure thing, king. Thanks for the hospitality.

117 **ACT THREE NARRATOR:** When they had heard the king they went on their way;

118 and lo, the star, which they had seen in the East, went before them, till it came

119 to rest over the place where the child was. And being warned in a dream not

120 to return to Herod, they departed to their own country by another way.

121

122 **"SING WE NOW OF CHRISTMAS" (CD # 7, MUSIC PAGE 42)**

                                      The Backward Christmas Pageant

Act Two

1   (**Sign Holder** *holds up "ACT TWO" card. Play optional music as the card is displayed.*)

2

3

4   **OPTIONAL MUSIC: "SHEPHERD'S MUSIC" (CD #8)**

5

6   (**Shepherd 1, Shepherd 2, extra shepherds (optional),** *and* **Angel** *move into place.*)

7

8   **ACT TWO NARRATOR:** And in that region there were shepherds out in the field,

9   keeping watch over their flock by night. And an angel of the Lord appeared

10   to them, and the glory of the Lord shone around them and they were filled

11   with fear. And the angel said to them, "Be not afraid, for behold, I bring you

12   good news of a great joy which will come to all the people; for to you is born

13   this day in the city of David a Savior, who is Christ the Lord. And this will be a

14   sign for you: you will find a babe wrapped in swaddling cloths and lying in a

15   manger." And suddenly there was with the angel a multitude of the heavenly

16   host praising God and saying, "Glory to God in the highest, and on earth,

17   peace, good will to all."

18

19 (**Sheep** *"baa" from narthex. A few sheep should slowly move to the chancel area and sit quietly*

20 *near the* **Shepherds.**)

21

22 **OPTIONAL: SHEEP SOUND EFFECT (CD #4)**

23

24 (*Fade sheep sounds as* **Shepherd 1** *speaks next line.*)

25

26 (**Rookie Shepherd** *dashes up the aisle, arriving at the chancel breathless.*)

27

28 **SHEPHERD 1:** Floyd! Where have you been?

29 **ROOKIE SHEPHERD:** (*Gasping*) I'm sorry . . . I'm late . . .

30 **SHEPHERD 1:** You *should* be sorry. First night on the job, and you're late?

31 **ROOKIE SHEPHERD:** (*Gasping*) I know—

32 **SHEPHERD 1:** You're not one of those people who think being a shepherd is easy,

33   are you?

34 **ROOKIE SHEPHERD:** (*Gasping*) No, sir . . .

SHEPHERD 1: It's not like we just sit up here, admiring the view, staring at the stars. Uh, uh. We *work* on this hillside. There are dozens of sheep out there, counting on us. If one of us isn't pulling his weight, we could have a disaster on our hands.

ROOKIE SHEPHERD: *(Gasping)* Yes, sir . . .

SHEPHERD 1: Remember the Shepherd's Credo: "On the hill, on time, on the job!"

SHEPHERD 2: Uh, chief?

SHEPHERD 1: What is it?

SHEPHERD 2: Time for dinner break.

SHEPHERD 1: OK, everybody! Chow time!

(All **Shepherds** *except* **Rookie Shepherd** *pull out paper bags and begin to mime eating.)*

ROOKIE SHEPHERD: Excuse me, could you spare some?

SHEPHERD 2: What?

ROOKIE SHEPHERD: *(Sheepishly)* I don't have any dinner.

SHEPHERD 2: You don't?

ROOKIE SHEPHERD: No, sir, you see I gave it to this young girl who looked like she needed it more than me.

SHEPHERD 2: Oh, never mind. Here. *(Passes sandwich to* **Rookie Shepherd***.)* I hope you like peanut butter and jelly.

ROOKIE SHEPHERD: *(Enthusiastically)* Yes sir, I love peanut butter and jelly!

ANGEL: *(From balcony or other visible place)* Be not afraid!

SHEPHERDS: *(Mouths full of peanut butter)* Mwuf, mwuf!

ANGEL: For I bring great tidings of great joy! For unto you is born this day a Savior, which is Christ the Lord!

SHEPHERDS: Mwuf, mwuf!

ANGEL: And this shall be a sign to you: you shall find the babe wrapped in swaddling clothes and lying in a manger.

SHEPHERDS: Mwuf, mwuf!

ANGEL CHORUS: Glory to God in the highest, and on earth, peace, good will to all!

SHEPHERD 1: Boy that was amazing!

SHEPHERD 2: There we were, in the presence of God's messenger, and we were all struck silent!

ROOKIE SHEPHERD: That peanut butter really sticks to the roof of your mouth, doesn't it?

SHEPHERD 1: Let us go to Bethlehem and see this thing of which the angel spoke.

SHEPHERD 2: What about the sheep?

74   **SHEPHERD 1:** Leave them. They're just sheep. What trouble can they get into?

75

76   (**Sheep** *bleat, wander offstage.*)

77

78   **OPTIONAL: SHEEP SOUND EFFECT (CD #4)**

79

80   (*Bring up sheep sounds and then fade.*)

81

82   **ACT TWO NARRATOR:** When the angels went away to heaven, the shepherds said

83   to one another, "Let us go over to Bethlehem and see this thing that has

84   hapened and which the Lord has made known to us." And they went with

85   haste, and found Mary and Joseph, and the babe lying in a manger.

86

87

88   **"RISE UP, SHEPHERD, AND FOLLOW" (CD #9, MUSIC PAGE 44)**

Act One
Scene 1

1   (**Sign Holder** *holds up "ACT ONE" card. Play optional music as the card is displayed.*)

2

3   🎵 **OPTIONAL MUSIC: "BETHLEHEM JOURNEY," SHORT VERSION**

4   **(CD #3)**

5

6   (**Joseph** *and* **Mary** *move into place.*)

7

8   **ACT ONE NARRATOR:** In the days of Herod, King of Judea, there was a priest
9   named Zechariah, whose wife was named Elizabeth. They were both righteous
10   before God. But they had no child, and both were advanced in years. In the
11   temple, there appeared to Zechariah an angel of the Lord who said to him,
12   "Do not be afraid, Zechariah, for your prayer is heard, and your wife
13   Elizabeth will bear a son, and you shall call his name John." And Zechariah
14   said, "How shall I know this? For I am an old man, and my wife is advanced in
15   years." And the angel answered him, "I am Gabriel, who stand in the presence
16   of God; and I was sent to speak to you, and to bring you good news. And,
17   behold, you will be silent and unable to speak until the day that these things
18   come to pass."

19   **JOSEPH:** I got the mail, Mary. Here's a letter for you.

20   **MARY:** Thanks, Joseph. How was everything in the shop today? (*Opens her letter and*
21   *begins to read.*)

22   **JOSEPH:** Oh, the usual. Sawing, hammering, sweeping. Then more sawing.
23   Sometimes, I wish things were a little different. Just one day after another, all
24   the same . . .

25   **MARY:** (*Interrupting*) I don't believe it!

26   **JOSEPH:** Mary, I really *do* wish that things were different.

27   **MARY:** No, this letter. It's from Elizabeth.

28   **JOSEPH:** Zechariah's wife?

29   **MARY:** Right. They're going to have a baby.

30   **JOSEPH:** A baby? At *their* age?

31   **MARY:** And that's not all. Zechariah can't speak.

32   **JOSEPH:** He can't speak? Not at all?

33   **MARY:** They think he saw a vision in the temple.

34   **JOSEPH:** Maybe he was thinking about midnight feedings.

                  The Backward Christmas Pageant

35 **MARY:** This is amazing. They have been praying for this for years.

36 **JOSEPH:** Well, I guess when God wants to do a miracle, you get a miracle. *(Looks at*
37 *mail, holds up green slip.)* Hey, a certified letter! I'll run down to the post office
38 and pick it up.

39
40 *(*Joseph *exits, as the* Angel *comes to the door and knocks.)*

41
42 **KNOCKING SOUND EFFECT (CD #10)**

43
44 *(*Mary *opens the door.)*

45
46 **ANGEL:** Greetings, favored one! The Lord is with you!

47 **MARY:** Are you sure you're not looking for my husband?

48 **ANGEL:** Do not be afraid, for you have found favor with God!

49 **MARY:** So . . . this is going to be good news, right?

50 **ANGEL:** You will conceive in your womb and bear a son, and you will name him
51 Jesus. He will be great and will be called the Son of the Most High, and the
52 Lord will give to him the throne of his ancestor David. He will reign over the
53 house of Jacob forever, and of his kingdom there will be no end.

54 **MARY:** How can this be?

55 **ANGEL:** The Holy Spirit will come upon you, and the power of the Most High will
56 overshadow you; therefore, the child to be born will be holy; he will be called
57 the Son of God. And now, your relative Elizabeth in her old age has also con-
58 ceived a son; for nothing is impossible with God.

59 **MARY:** Here am I, the servant of the Lord. Let it be with me according to your
60 word.

61
62 *(The* Angel *exits.* Joseph *enters.)*

63
64 **JOSEPH:** Good thing I picked up this letter. There's going to be a census, and . . .
65 is something wrong?

66 **MARY:** *(Slowly, as if stunned)* Joseph, you know how an angel told Elizabeth and
67 Zechariah that they're having a baby, even though they're quite old?

68 **JOSEPH:** Uh, yes.

69 **MARY:** *(Beginning to get excited)* Well, an angel just came here and told me that I will
70 have a baby who will be the Son of God.

71 **JOSEPH:** How can this be?

72 **MARY:** I asked the same question. The angel said nothing is impossible with God.

73 **JOSEPH:** First, I'm really happy. Second, we have a problem.

74 **MARY:** What's the problem?

75 **JOSEPH:** This letter. They're doing a census.

76 **MARY:** Why is that a problem?

77 **JOSEPH:** We have to go back to my hometown—Bethlehem.

78 **MARY:** I like Bethlehem. When do we leave?

79 **JOSEPH:** In about nine months.

80

81 *(Mary and Joseph slowly turn to look at one another.)*

82

83 **MARY and JOSEPH:** Uh, oh.

84 **JOSEPH:** I sure hope that angel was right about the "nothing is impossible" part.

85 **ACT ONE NARRATOR:** In the sixth month the angel Gabriel was sent from God to
86 a city of Galilee named Nazareth, to a virgin betrothed to a man whose name
87 was Joseph, of the house of David; and the virgin's name was Mary. And he
88 came to her and said, "Hail, O favored one, the Lord is with you!" But she was
89 greatly troubled at the saying, and considered in her mind what sort of greet-
90 ing this might be. And the angel said to her, "Do not be afraid Mary, for you
91 have found favor with God. And behold, you will conceive in your womb and
92 bear a son, and you shall call his name Jesus."

93

94

95 **"O COME, ALL YE FAITHFUL" (CD #11, MUSIC PAGE 46)**

96

97 *(During the singing,* **Rookie Shepherd** *moves into the Act 1, Scene 2 position on the floor,*
98 *adding a few extra large rags around the body as desired to create the effect of a large rag pile.*
100 **Mary** *and* **Joseph** *may move slowly across the chancel to mime their travel to Bethlehem.)*

The Backward Christmas Pageant

Act One
Scene 2

1 **ACT ONE NARRATOR:** In those days a decree went out from Caesar Augustus that
2   all the world should be enrolled. This was the first enrollment, when
3   Quirinius was governor of Syria. And all went to be enrolled, each to his own
4   city. And Joseph also went up from Galilee, from the city of Nazareth, to
5   Judea, to the city of David, which is called Bethlehem, because he was of the
6   house and lineage of David, to be enrolled with Mary, his betrothed, who was
7   with child.

8

9 **STABLE ANIMAL SOUND EFFECTS (CD #12)**

10

11 *(Fade sound effects to a very soft level during the beginning of the dialogue, gradually fading*
12 *away by the time* **Mary** *sits.)*

13

14 **JOSEPH:** So, what do you think?
15 **MARY:** It's not the honeymoon suite.
16 **JOSEPH:** It fits our budget.
17 **MARY:** I'm sure it will do fine.

18

19 (**Mary** *sits on the pile of rags, which turns out to be a sleeping* **Rookie Shepherd**.)

20

21 **MARY:** I'm sorry. Are you all right?
22 **ROOKIE SHEPHERD:** *(Stands up.)* I'm fine. Oh, man, I'm late for work! And it's my
23 first night on the job! I've just been promoted from stable boy to shepherd!
24 **JOSEPH:** Congratulations. Before you go, is there someplace around here we can
25 get dinner?
26 **ROOKIE SHEPHERD:** No, the restaurant at the inn stops serving at ten. *(Picks up*
27 *paper "lunch bag" and offers it to* **Mary**.*)* But, here, take mine.
28 **MARY:** No, we couldn't.
29 **ROOKIE SHEPHERD:** It's OK. Hope you like peanut better and jelly.

30

31 (**Mary** *takes the bag.* **Rookie Shepherd** *quickly runs offstage.)*

32

33 **MARY:** *(Toward the retreating* **Rookie Shepherd***)* Thank you!

34   **JOSEPH:** *(Waves toward **Rookie Shepherd**.)* Good night!

35

36

37   "O LITTLE TOWN OF BETHLEHEM" (CD #13, MUSIC PAGE 48)

     The Backward Christmas Pageant

Epilogue

1   **NARRATOR 1:** And while they were there, the time came for her to be delivered.
2   And she gave birth to her firstborn son and wrapped him in swaddling cloths,
3   and laid him in a manger, because there was no room for them in the inn.

4

5   🎵 **"AWAY IN A MANGER" (CD #14, MUSIC PAGE 50)**

6

7   **JOSEPH:** Baby fall asleep again?
8   **MARY:** Yes. I'm glad you thought of putting him in the manger.
9   **JOSEPH:** How was the sandwich?
10   **MARY:** Perfect. What a wonderful gift. Stuck to the roof of my mouth a little, though.
11   **JOSEPH:** It's hard to believe.
12   **MARY:** What? Peanut butter?
13   **JOSEPH:** Everything the angel said.
14   **MARY:** Oh, I can believe it. There are moments that change everything. This is one
15   of them.

16

17   (**Shepherds** *and* **Rookie Shepherd** *enter.*)

18

19   **OPTIONAL: "SHEPHERD'S MUSIC" (CD #8)**

20

21   *(Fade music as* **Shepherds** *take their places.)*

22

23   **NARRATOR 2:** When the angels went away to heaven, the shepherds said to one
24   another, "Let us go over to Bethlehem and see this thing that has happened
25   and which the Lord has made known to us." And they went with haste, and
26   found Mary and Joseph, and the babe lying in a manger. And when they saw it
27   they made known the saying which had been told them concerning this child;
28   and all who heard it wondered at what the shepherds told them. And the
29   shepherds returned, glorifying and praising God for all they had heard and
30   seen, as it had been told them.
31   **SHEPHERD 1:** Is this the child the angels told us about?
32   **MARY:** Yes.
33   **ROOKIE SHEPHERD:** *(Looking around)* I love what you've done with this place.

34 (**Wise People** *enter.*)

35

36 **OPTIONAL MUSIC: "BETHLEHEM JOURNEY" SHORT VERSION (CD #3)**

37

38 *(Fade music as the* **Wise People** *take their places.)*

39

40 **NARRATOR 1:** When the Wise People had heard the king they went on their way;
41 and lo, the star which they had seen in the East went before them, till it came
42 to rest over the place where the child was. When they saw the star, they
43 rejoiced exceedingly with great joy; and going into the house they saw the
44 child with Mary his mother, and they fell down and worshiped him.

45 **WISE PERSON 1:** Excuse me. We are Wise People from the East. We are here to
46 worship the newborn king.

47 **JOSEPH:** *(To* **Wise Person 4***)* I thought you had a soccer game.

48 **WISE PERSON 4:** I wanted to see how the story ends.

49 **JOSEPH:** This is one of those stories that never ends.

50 **NARRATOR 1:** And Mary kept all these things, pondering them in her heart.

51 **MARY:** *This* will change everything.

52 **NARRATOR 2:** From now on, it will be hard to remember what life was like before
53 this happened.

54 **NARRATOR 1:** This *will* change everything.

55 **NARRATOR 2:** All fear and all terror will be as nothing compared to the love and
56 hope in the face of one small baby.

57 **NARRATOR 1:** This will change *everything*.

58 **NARRATOR 2:** This is the moment of God's grace.

59 **NARRATOR 1:** And this moment is forever!

60

61

62 **MEDLEY: "ON THIS DAY" / "JOY TO THE WORLD" (CD #15,**
63 **MUSIC PAGE 52)**

         The Backward Christmas Pageant

Song Texts

Track #2

We Three Kings

1. We three kings of Orient are;
   bearing gifts we traverse afar,
   field and fountain, moor and mountain,
   following yonder star.

Refrain

   O star of wonder, star of light,
   star with royal beauty bright,
   westward leading, still proceeding,
   guide us to thy perfect light.

2. Born a King on Bethlehem's plain,
   gold I bring to crown him again,
   King forever, ceasing never,
   over us all to reign.

Refrain

3. Frankincense to offer have I;
   incense owns a Deity nigh;
   prayer and praising, voices raising,
   worshiping God on high.

Refrain

4. Myrrh is mine; its bitter perfume
   breathes a life of gathering gloom;
   sorrowing, sighing, bleeding, dying,
   sealed in the stone-cold tomb.

Refrain

5. Glorious now behold him arise;
   King and God and sacrifice:
   Alleluia, Alleluia,
   sounds through the earth and skies.

Refrain

Track #6

Good Christian Friends, Rejoice

1. Good Christian friends, rejoice
   with heart and soul and voice;
   now ye hear of endless bliss: News, news!
   Jesus Christ was born for this!
   He hath opened heaven's door,
   and ye are blest forevermore.
   Christ was born for this,
   Christ was born for this!

2. Good Christian friends, rejoice
   with heart and soul and voice;
   now ye need not fear the grave:
      News, news!
   Jesus Christ was born to save!
   Calls you one and calls you all
   to gain his everlasting hall.
   Christ was born to save,
   Christ was born to save!

Sing We Now of Christmas    *Track #7*

1. From the eastern country
   came the kings afar,
   bearing gifts to Bethlehem,
   guided by the star.

Refrain

   Sing we Noel,
   the King is born, Noel!
   Sing we now of Christmas,
   sing we now Noel!

2. Gold and myrrh they took there,
   gifts of greatest price;
   there was never a stable
   so like paradise.

Refrain

Track #9

Rise Up, Shepherd, and Follow

1. There's a star in the East on Christmas
      morn;
   rise up, shepherd, and follow;
   it will lead to the place where the Christ
      was born;
   rise up, shepherd, and follow.

Refrain

   Follow, follow, rise up shepherd, and
      follow,
   follow the star of Bethlehem.
   Rise up, shepherd, and follow.

2. If you take good heed to the angel's
      words;
   rise up, shepherd, and follow;
   you'll forget your flocks, you'll forget
      your herds;
   rise up, shepherd, and follow.

Refrain   *Track #11*

O Come, All Ye Faithful

1. O come, all ye faithful, joyful and
      triumphant,
   O come ye, O come ye, to Bethlehem.
   Come and behold him, born the King
      of angels.

Refrain

   O come, let us adore him, O come, let
      us adore him,
   O come, let us adore him, Christ the
      Lord.

2. Sing, choirs of angels, sing in exultation;
   O sing, all ye citizens of heaven above!
   Glory to God, all glory in the highest.

Refrain

         The Backward Christmas Pageant

O Little Town of Bethlehem

Track #13

1. O little town of Bethlehem, how still we
      see thee lie;
   above thy deep and dreamless sleep the
      silent stars go by.
   Yet in thy dark streets shineth the
      everlasting light;
   the hopes and fears of all the years are
      met in thee tonight.

2. For Christ is born of Mary, and
      gathered all above;
   while mortals sleep, the angels keep
      their watch of wondering love.
   O morning stars together, proclaim the
      holy birth,
   and praises sing to God the King, and
      peace to all on earth!

3. O holy Child of Bethlehem, descend to
      us, we pray;
   cast out our sin, and enter in, be born
      in us today.
   We hear the Christmas angels the great
      glad tidings tell;
   O come to us, abide with us, our Lord
      Emmanuel!

Away in a Manger

Track #14

1. Away in a manger, no crib for a bed,
      the little Lord Jesus laid down his sweet
      head.
   The stars in the sky looked down where
      he lay,
   the little Lord Jesus asleep on the hay.

2. The cattle are lowing, the baby awakes,
      but little Lord Jesus, no crying he
      makes;
   I love thee, Lord Jesus, look down from
      the sky
   and stay by my cradle till morning is
      nigh.

3. Be near me, Lord Jesus, I ask thee to
      stay
   close by me forever, and love me, I pray;
   bless all the dear children in thy tender
      care,
   and fit us for heaven to live with thee
      there.

Medley: On This Day/Joy to the World

On This Day Earth Shall Ring

1. On this day earth shall ring with the
      song children sing
   to the Lord, Christ our King, born on
      earth to save us;
   him the Father gave us.
   Ideo, ideo, ideo gloria in excelsis Deo!

Joy to the World

2. Joy to the world, the Lord is come!
   Let earth receive her King;
   let every heart prepare him room,
   and heaven and nature sing, and
      heaven and nature sing,
   and heaven, and heaven, and nature
      sing.

3. He rules the world with truth and grace,
   and makes the nations prove
   the glories of his righteousness,
   and wonders of his love, and wonders
      of his love,
   and wonders, wonders of his love.

On This Day Earth Shall Ring

4. On this day angels sing; with their song
      earth shall ring,
   praising Christ, heaven's King, born on
      earth to save us;
   peace and love he gave us.
   Ideo, ideo, ideo gloria in excelsis Deo!
   Ideo, ideo, ideo gloria in excelsis Deo!

Script Notes

PROLOGUE

✩ **You may want to keep the title a secret.** In theater, it's always good to have the element of surprise on your side. In this case, it might be a good idea not to divulge the actual name of this pageant until after it has begun. In advance publicity, and even in the bulletin handed out as the congregation arrives (if you do one), call it "This Year's Christmas Pageant," or something equally noncommittal. The idea of doing the Christmas story backward is unusual enough that it's a bonus for the audience if they don't know what's coming. When we produced this pageant, I had the notion of handing out bulletins with a phony title and the usual "Act 1–Act 2–Act 3" sequence printed on them. When the narrator announced "The Backward Christmas Pageant!" I had the ushers tear large sheets of paper in the back of the sanctuary, and then appear with new bulletins that looked like they had been cut and pasted in a rush. The ushers tried to hand them out to the congregation, but everyone waved them off. The congregants already had bulletins and believed that they didn't need another. I thought it was a good idea, and if anyone can make it work, let the rest of us know. For those of you who have projection capabilities, ask your technology person to create a process for the "change" to happen on screen as the congregation watches.

✩ **"I think it's a soccer game."** This is as close as we come to social satire. I'm sure there is some child-participant sport that competes with worship in your community. In ours, it's soccer. This line works in part because, later on, when the wise people reveal their gifts, it's a clever visual to see a soccer ball where one expects to see myrrh. Pick the sport that intrudes the most on worship in your community, and find a prop that fits. For instance, if it's hockey, a goalie mask is a bigger, more humorous image than a puck.

✩ **"What's on second? Who's on first?"** This is a play on a very old comedy routine by Abbott and Costello. Enjoy it. If you've never heard of them (or the "Who's On First" routine), refer to one of the many Abbott and Costello websites.

ACT THREE

✩ **Signs and sign holders.** Each act begins with the display of a large sign to remind the audience of the new order of the acts. Make the sign large enough to be seen and easily read. You could ask your sign holder to stand still on one side of the chancel or to move across the chancel holding the sign. Music is included on the CD to use as the sign is held and the cast moves into place. Fade the music when your cast is ready to begin.

✩ **Let's talk sheep.** The sheep appear in all three acts, which seems to contradict our "one actor, one act" rule. There are two ways to deal with this: (1) Allocate different sheep to each act, rehearsing them as you would the rest of the cast; or (2) Use the same flock of sheep in each act, realizing that they don't have any lines aside from the occasional "baa" or other animal sound. At the first rehearsal, they would rehearse with the Act One (Mary and Joseph) group, as that's where they do most of their bleating. At the second rehearsal, the director will have to work them into the other two acts. The easiest way to do this is to have an assistant director assigned to guide them. This assistant director would know when and where their entrances are, and when they're supposed to make noise. It would be altogether fitting and proper for this assistant director to be dressed as a shepherd. When we did this pageant, we cast our first and second grade church school classes as sheep, called them "The Livestock Chorale," and gave them their own song in the manger scene. "Away in the Manger" is offered as a possibility in this publication. There is a Sheep Sound Effect included on the CD, which you can use if your sheep need a gentle reminder of when to "baa."

☆ **How many Wise People?** The script calls for four wise people. I never cast only three, because the Bible never says how many there were; our notion that there were three comes from the number of gifts. Since the wise people never speak to one another, you could actually get away with only one speaking the lines, except for the "Gold, Frankincense, Myrrh!" presentation, where each of them has to be able to speak one word. On the other hand, you could

have more speaking parts, if you're blessed with a big cast.

☆ **Point and look with telescope.** This "tableau" gag is intended to poke fun at ourselves and our sometimes overly dramatic renditions of biblical scenes. Young casts like being dramatic, if they know the audience will find it funny.

☆ **"Myrrh. Oops!"** Once the soccer ball (or other piece of sports equipment is revealed), have the prop person come onstage in a dead run from as far offstage as possible. In our pageant, the prop person was the only cast member not dressed in pageant costume; ours wore a T-shirt, jeans, sneakers, and a headset, to look like he or she was supposed to be backstage. I had our prop person run onstage, take the ball, run off, run back on with the myrrh, and run back, while the Wise Person involved in the gag stands frozen.

☆ **Herod's lint.** Cotton balls stuck onto Velcro dots. The more, the merrier.

ACT TWO

☆ **Rookie Shepherd.** Here's the other exception to the "one actor, one act" rule: Rookie Shepherd appears in the second scene of Act One. At the first rehearsal, Rookie Shepherd will rehearse with the Act Two cast. Somewhere in your rehearsal schedule, you have to find a time to insert Rookie Shepherd into Act One.

☆ **Shepherds.** If you are producing this as a full-scale production you may want to have some extra shepherds for effect. You could divide the Shepherd 1 and Shepherd 2 lines into several shepherd parts. The shepherds could be a specific age level children's group or a choir if desired. The group could sing "Rise Up, Shepherd, and Follow" or another selection before leaving their places at the end of Act 2.

✩ **Angel Chorus.** I've had a little success with the congregation doing the "peace on earth" line. Print the line in the bulletin, and tell the congregation before the pageant that you will be putting them to work—sort of an interactive pageant experience. One of the cast members is assigned the task of cuing the audience with a silent "one, two, three" count, and then pointing. Rehearsing this before the pageant is a good way to warm up the congregation. If you have projection capabilities you could also put the line on-screen.

ACT ONE

✩ **The mail.** Don't use any more mail than you have to, since Mary and Joseph each only need one letter. We did fine with a FedEx envelope (which got an unexpected laugh). Use a real certified mail slip, if possible. Whatever you use, make it large enough to be seen by the audience.

✩ **The Angel knocking on the door**. The Angel will need to practice knocking on an invisible door, which Mary will need to practice opening. If you are using the Sound Effect on the CD, the sound person will need to be included in the rehearsal too.

EPILOGUE

✩ **"This will change everything."** As mentioned before, this is the topic sentence of the pageant. The finale is a slow winding down the antic spirit to a liturgical coda. If you've done it right, the congregation will be with you on this.

We Three Kings

WORDS: John H. Hopkins, Jr.
MUSIC: John H. Hopkins, Jr.; transcribed by Allen Tuten
Transcription © 2003 Abingdon Press, admin. by The Copyright Co., Nashville, TN 37212

far,   field and foun - tain, moor and moun - tain,
gain,   King for - ev - er, ceas - ing nev - er,
nigh;   prayer and prais - ing, voic - es rais - ing,
gloom;   sor - rowing, sigh - ing, bleed - ing, dy - ing,
fice: Al - le - lu - ia, Al - le - lu - ia,

fol - low - ing yon - der star. _____
o - ver us all to reign. _____
wor - ship - ing God on high. _____
sealed in the stone - cold tomb. _____
sounds through the earth and skies. _____

O _____

—   star of won - der, star of light,

38

Good Christian Friends, Rejoice

WORDS: 14th cent. Latin; trans. by John Mason Neale
MUSIC: German melody; transcribed by Allen Tuten

Sing We Now of Christmas

WORDS: Trad. French carol
MUSIC: Trad. French carol; transcribed by Allen Tuten
Transcription © 2003 Abingdon Press, admin. by The Copyright Co., Nashville, TN 37212

Rise Up, Shepherd, and Follow

WORDS: African American spiritual
MUSIC: African American spiritual; transcribed by Allen Tuten
Transcription © 2003 Abingdon Press, admin. by The Copyright Co., Nashville, TN 37212

O Come, All Ye Faithful

WORDS: John F. Wade; trans. Frederick Oakeley and others
MUSIC: John F. Wade; transcribed by Allen Tuten

Transcription © 2003 Abingdon Press, admin. by The Copyright Co., Nashville, TN 37212

O Little Town of Bethlehem

WORDS: Phillips Brooks
MUSIC: Phillips Brooks; transcribed by Allen Tuten
Transcription © 2003 Abingdon Press, admin. by The Copyright Co., Nashville, TN 37212

in thy dark streets shin - eth the ev - er - last - ing light; the
morn - ing stars to - geth - er, pro - claim the ho - ly birth, and
hear the Christ-mas an - gels the great glad tid - ings tell; O

hopes and fears of all the years are met in thee to - night.
prais - es sing to God the King, and peace to all on earth.
come to us, a - bide with us, our Lord Em - man - u -

2. For el!
3. O

Away in a Manger

WORDS: Anonymous
MUSIC: James R. Murray; transcribed by Allen Tuten

Medley: On This Day/Joy to the World

WORDS: *Piae Cantiones*; trans. by Jane M. Joseph
MUSIC: Melody from *Piae Cantiones*; transcribed by Allen Tuten

*WORDS: Isaac Watts
MUSIC: Arr. from G. F. Handel by Lowell Mason; transcribed by Allen Tuten

Transcription © 2003 Abingdon Press, admin. by The Copyright Co., Nashville, TN 37212

Notes

The Backward Christmas Pageant CD Track List

#1   Bethlehem Journey (Long Version)

#2   We Three Kings*
       Arr. © 2003 Abingdon Press, admin. by The Copyright Company, Nashville, TN

#3   Bethlehem Journey (Short Version)

#4   SFX: Sheep

#5   SFX: King Herod's Entrance

#6   Good Christian Friends, Rejoice*
       Arr. © 2003 Abingdon Press, admin. by The Copyright Company, Nashville, TN

#7   Sing We Now of Christmas*
       Arr. © 2003 Abingdon Press, admin. by The Copyright Company, Nashville, TN

#8   Shepherd's Music

#9   Rise Up, Shepherd, and Follow*
       Arr. © 2003 Abingdon Press, admin. by The Copyright Company, Nashville, TN

#10   SFX: Door Knock

#11   O Come, All Ye Faithful*
       Arr. © 2003 Abingdon Press, admin. by The Copyright Company, Nashville, TN

#12   SFX: Stable Sounds

#13   O Little Town of Bethlehem*
       Arr. © 2003 Abingdon Press, admin. by The Copyright Company, Nashville, TN

#14   Away in a Manger*
       Arr. © 2003 Abingdon Press, admin. by The Copyright Company, Nashville, TN

#15   Medley: On This Day / Joy to the World*
       Arr. © 2003 Abingdon Press, admin. by The Copyright Company, Nashville, TN

Tracks 2, 6, 7, 9, 11, 13, 14, and 15 are in split-track format.

Permission is granted to purchaser to reproduce this page for use with the CD.